Alicia Vikander Adult Coloring Book

Famous Tomb Raider and Academy Award Winner, Hot Actress and Forbes Top Youth Actress Inspired Adult Coloring Book

Elizabet Hathorn

"Det känns inte
som att det borde
vara lagligt"

ELLE

courtnaypinheiro
Chef's Warehouse B... >

Follow

Terminal 5
smartecarte
smartecarte
smartecarte

Entertainment
WEEKLY

VENO
ROMA